Patterns

David Kirkby

First published in Great Britain by Heinemann Library
an imprint of Heinemann Publishers (Oxford) Ltd
Halley Court, Jordan Hill, Oxford OX2 8EJ

MADRID ATHENS PARIS
FLORENCE PRAGUE WARSAW
PORTSMOUTH NH CHICAGO SAO PAULO
SINGAPORE TOKYO MELBOURNE AUCKLAND
IBADAN GABORONE JOHANNESBURG

© Heinemann Publishers (Oxford) Ltd

Designed by The Point
Cover design by Pinpoint Design
Printed in China
Produced by Mandarin Offset
99 98 97 96 95
10 9 8 7 6 5 4 3 2 1

ISBN 0431 06898 4

British Library Cataloguing in Publication Data
Kirkby, David
Patterns. - (Maths Live Series)
I. Title II. Series
516.15

Acknowledgements
The author and publisher wish to acknowledge, with thanks,
the following photographic sources:
NHPA pp8, 10, 14; Roger Scruton p12; Zefa p6; Trevor Clifford p18, *32 centre*, 34;
Courtesy of Fired Earth p14; Bruce Coleman p18; RNIB p27.

The publishers would also like to thank the following for the kind loan of equipment:
NES Arnold Ltd; Polydron International Ltd.

Note to reader: words in **bold** in the text are explained in the glossary on page 44.

CONTENTS

1 PATTERNS IN MATHEMATICS

The study of **patterns** is at the heart of mathematics.
If you can spot patterns, this will help you to recognize
relationships in mathematics. Mathematics involves a
study of things like number, shape, space, position and
graphs. Patterns occur in all of these.

We can see different patterns all around us.

This garden path uses patterns in shapes to create a neat
and attractive design.

A builder uses different ways of arranging the bricks in
the walls of a building. The arrangement creates a neat
regular pattern.

Patterns occur in nature and many relate to mathematical shapes.

It is important to be able to recognize a pattern so that it can be extended. For example, the number sequence 1, 3, 5, 7, 9 . . . can be continued when the pattern is recognized.
What are the next two numbers in the sequence?

CHALLENGE:

What are the next two numbers in each of these number sequences?

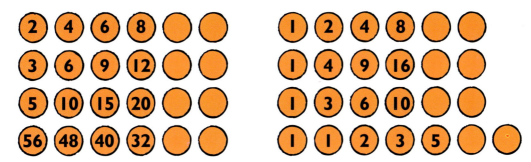

CHALLENGE:

- Copy the triangle pattern opposite.
- Can you write the next two rows of the triangle?
- Do you notice any patterns in the numbers in the triangle?

Pascal, a French mathematician, created this number pattern. It is known as Pascal's Triangle.

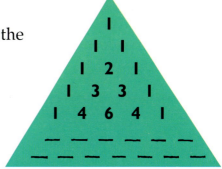

5

2 REFLECTIONS

Look at this picture. In the water you can see an upside-down image of the building. This image is called a **reflection**.

A reflected image can be used to create a pattern.

TO DO:

- Place a dice in front of two mirrors which are hinged together with tape.
- When you look at the reflections, how many dice can you see?
- Change the angle of the mirrors. What is the largest number of dice you can see?
- How many spots can you see?

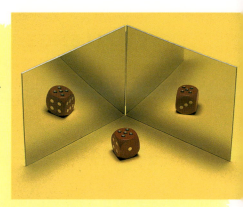

CHALLENGE:

Draw the reflection of words about a mirror line

- Write a word in capital letters.
- Imagine a mirror line drawn horizontally below the word, and try to draw the word's reflection.
- Do the same for a mirror line drawn vertically at the end of the word.

- Write the reflection of your name.
- Use a mirror to check that it is an accurate reflection.

By placing a mirror in different positions on this shape, it is possible to create different patterns.

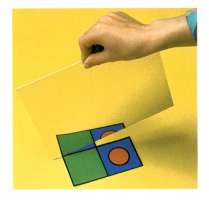
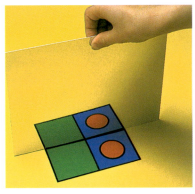

Look at the pattern made by placing the mirror as shown in the picture.

CHALLENGE:

You need a mirror.

- Place the mirror on the shape at the top of the page.
- Where should you place the mirror so that when you look through it you can see each of these patterns?

TO DO:

- Draw a square and colour it.
- Place a mirror on the square in different positions.
- Can you make these shapes?
- What other shapes can you make?

3 ROTATIONS

We are always using our hands to turn things. We turn the control knob on the cooker to turn up the heat. We turn the lid on a jar of coffee to open the jar. These turns are all examples of **rotations**. Rotations occur about a central point. For example, the centre of the lid stays in the same position as the lid is rotated. This central point is called the **centre of rotation**.

The sails of a windmill rotate in the wind. The centre of rotation is at the centre of the meeting point of the sails.

The picture below shows the position of a shape as it is rotated in a **clockwise** direction. At each stage, the shape has been rotated through a quarter turn or one **right angle**.

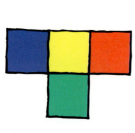 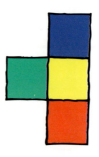 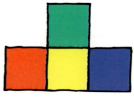 

TO DO:

Draw each of these shapes to show how they look when rotated through one, then two, then three and finally four right angles.

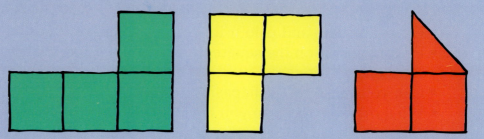

8

If two shapes are identical in size and shape, they are called **congruent** shapes. For example, shapes D and G are congruent because one is a rotation of the other.

CHALLENGE:

- There are five other congruent pairs of shapes. Can you find them?
- Which shape is the odd one out?

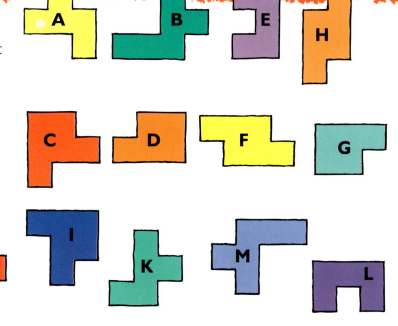

TO DO:

Make a rotating paper windmill

- Start with a square piece of paper.
- Draw straight lines along the diagonals.
- Colour a measured distance along each of these lines from each corner.
- Cut along these coloured lines. Fold each point to the centre of the square, then stick.
- Push a pin through the centre on to a straw or stick, then rotate your windmill.

4 LINE SYMMETRY

A shape in which one side is a reflection of the other side is said to have **line symmetry**. This is also called **reflective symmetry**. If a shape has line symmetry, we say that it is **symmetrical**. The straight line which divides the two symmetrical halves is called the **line of symmetry**.

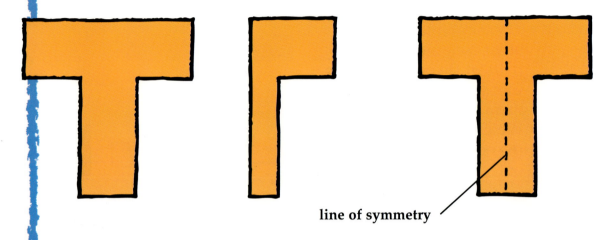

line of symmetry

This T-shape is symmetrical. It has been folded so that one half fits exactly on to the other half, then opened out. The folded line is the line of symmetry.

There are many examples of line symmetry in nature. Look at the pattern on each wing of the butterfly. The pattern on one side is a reflection of the pattern on the other.

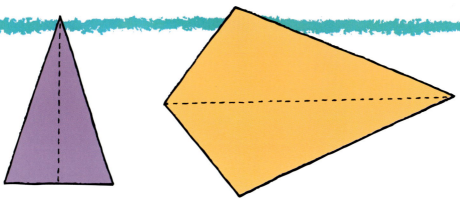

Some mathematical shapes are symmetrical. For example, the **isosceles triangle** and **kite** are both symmetrical. The dotted lines show the lines of symmetry.

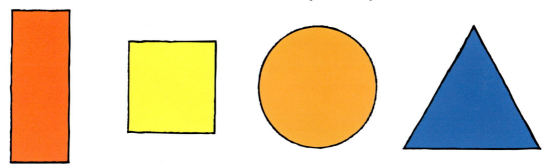

Some shapes have more than one line of symmetry. The rectangle has 2 lines of symmetry, the square has 4, and the **equilateral triangle** has 3.
The circle has a lot more. Where are these lines of symmetry?

TO DO:

Make some symmetrical shapes

 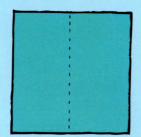  

- Start with a piece of paper, and fold it in half.
- Draw a shape alongside the fold.
- Cut along the drawn shape.
- Open it out. You have created a symmetrical shape.
- Make some different symmetrical shapes.

5 ROTATIONAL SYMMETRY

If an object is rotated through one complete turn, and in doing so, makes its own image more than once, then it is said to have **rotational symmetry**.

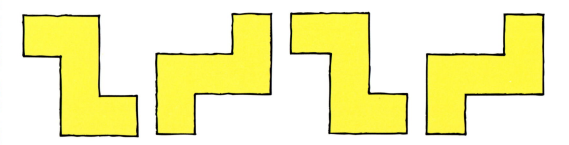

This shape has been rotated clockwise through quarter turns at each stage. It makes its own image after a half turn, and again after the full turn. As it makes its own image more than once, it has rotational symmetry.

The cartwheel has rotational symmetry. It makes its own image several times in one revolution. *How many times?*

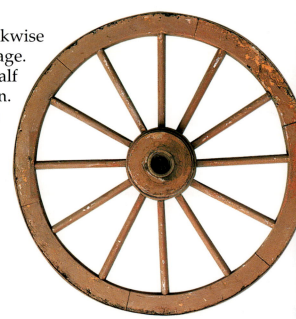

CHALLENGE:

Four of these six shapes have rotational symmetry. Which ones?

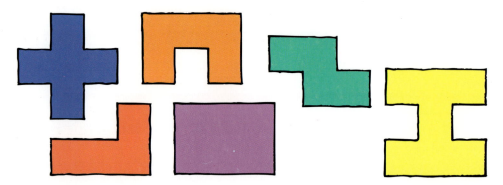

When a shape with rotational symmetry is rotated about its centre, the number of times it fits into its own image is called its **order of rotational symmetry**.

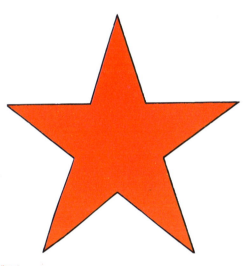

In one complete rotation, the star makes its own image five times. So the star has rotational symmetry of order 5.

CHALLENGE:

Here are some shapes with rotational symmetry.
What is the order of rotational symmetry for each shape?

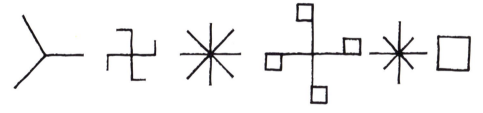

TO DO:

Crosswords can have rotational symmetry.

- Make your own crossword pattern with rotational symmetry by shading an 9 x 9 square.
- Write words as a solution to the puzzle, then invent their clues.
- Give your puzzle to a friend to solve.

TILING PATTERNS

Wall tiles and floor tiles can be arranged to make different patterns.

We can make our own tiles by colouring a set of squares.

TO DO:

Cut out six identical squares, then colour one half of each of them like this:

Arrange two of your tiles to make these patterns:

Put four tiles together to make these patterns:

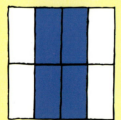 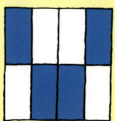 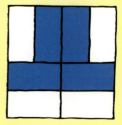 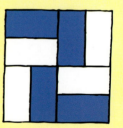

- Which of these patterns have line symmetry?
- Which have rotational symmetry?

CHALLENGE:

Using all six of your tiles, can you make five different patterns which all have line symmetry?

With sets of these tiles, it is possible to make these two-tile patterns:

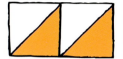  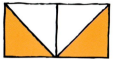 

and these four-tile patterns:

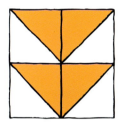 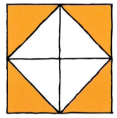 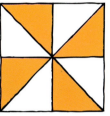 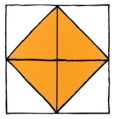

Interesting patterns can be made by using combinations of both tiles:

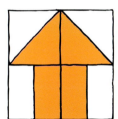 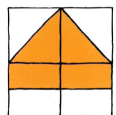  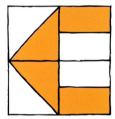

With sets of these tiles, you can make many different patterns.

Here are some four-tile examples:

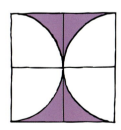 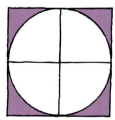 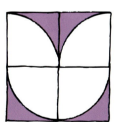 

TO DO:

- Invent your own tile and make a set.
- Create your own two-tile and four-tile patterns.

7 TESSELLATIONS

If a set of shapes can fit together snugly without leaving any gaps, they are said to **tessellate**. Some shapes tessellate by themselves.

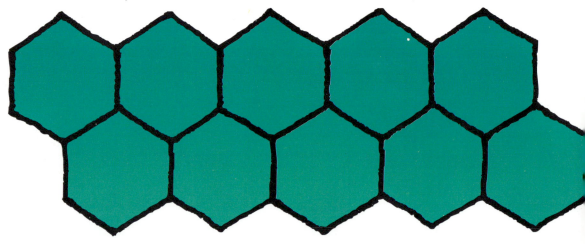

Here you can see that regular **hexagons** tessellate. There are no gaps between the joined hexagons.

There are examples of tessellating patterns in nature. The bees' honeycomb shows patterns of tessellating regular hexagons.

Regular **pentagons** will not tessellate on their own. No matter how you try to fit them together, there are always spaces between them.

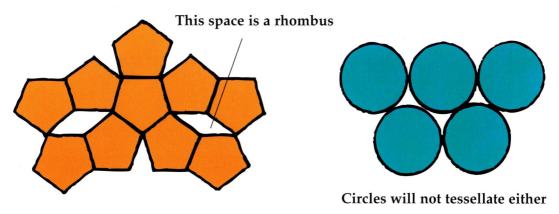

This space is a rhombus

Circles will not tessellate either

Tessellating patterns can be created by combining sets of two or three different shapes.

What shapes have been used in these tessellations?

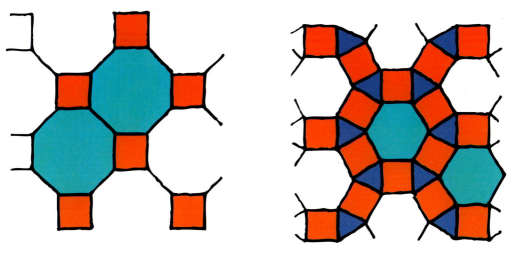

 TO DO:

- Draw any triangle on card.
- Cut it out, and use it as a template to make lots of other triangles the same size.
- Fit your triangles together so that they tessellate. This illustrates that any triangle will tessellate.
- Now repeat the activity for any four-sided shape (quadrilateral).

8 SPIRALS

Spirals are found everywhere. You may have seen a spiral staircase, or slid down a spiral helter-skelter. The thread of a screw is spiral shaped.

Many animals and plants have spiral shapes.

TO DO:

Draw a spiral
You need a pencil and a reel of cotton.

- Tie a pencil to the end of the cotton.
- Keep the reel fixed firmly on the paper, and the pencil upright.
- Then draw your spiral.

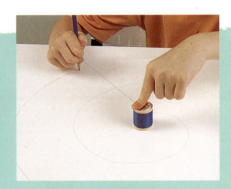

TO DO:

- Draw a spiral line on a sheet of paper, then cut along the line.
- Lift up the centre of the paper to make a spiral.

  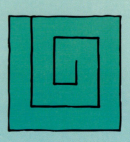 

Number spirals are created by writing numbers, in order, in a spiral arrangement on a square grid. Look carefully to see how this grid has been numbered.

50	51	52	53	54	55	56	57
49	26	27	28	29	30	31	58
48	25	10	11	12	13	32	59
47	24	9	2	3	14	33	60
46	23	8	1	4	15	34	61
45	22	7	6	5	16	35	62
44	21	20	19	18	17	36	63
43	42	41	40	39	38	37	64

What pattern do the odd numbers make? What about the even numbers?

What pattern do the square numbers make? What about the multiples of 4?

Do you notice any patterns along diagonal lines, along horizontal lines or along vertical lines?

CHALLENGE:

Make an Archimedean Spiral

- Draw a set of concentric circles (circles with the same centre), with the **radius** increasing by 0.5 cm each time.
- Draw two **diameters** at right angles to each other.
- Starting at the smallest circle, and marking a point where it meets a diameter, move round 90° clockwise and mark a point on the next smallest circle where it meets a diameter.
- Continue like this until you reach the outer circle.
- Join these marks to make a spiral.
- Cut out the spiral.

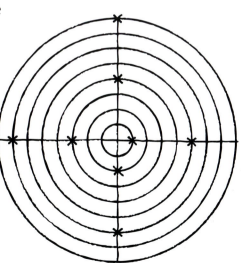

This is known as an Archimedean Spiral because the Greek mathematician, Archimedes, was the first person to make a detailed study of it.

9 STARS

Star shapes contain different mathematical patterns. They are described by their number of points.

Each star has both line symmetry and rotational symmetry. A 5-pointed star, for example, has rotational symmetry of order 5.

Stars can be drawn by joining the diagonals of a **regular polygon**. The most common example of this is the 5-pointed star, drawn inside a regular pentagon. It is called a **pentagram**.

TO DO:

Make a 4-pointed star

You need some large square pieces of paper.
- Fold one in half, then in half again.
- Draw two lines across the folded corner as shown below.
- Cut along the lines, open out the paper, and see what shape you have made.

Experiment with different cuts to make a collection of 4-pointed stars.

Regular polygons can be arranged to surround a star shape. *For each surrounding, what shapes have been used, and how many points has each star?*

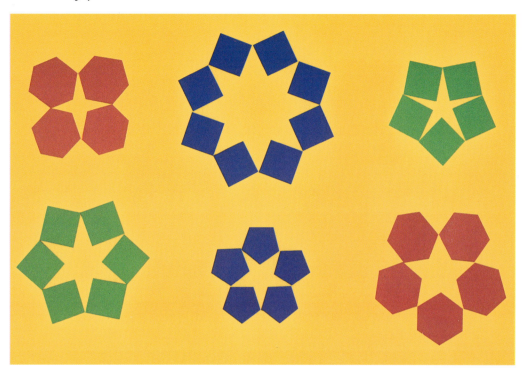

TO DO:

Make a star from two regular hexagons

- Use a template to draw two regular hexagons on card. Cut them out.
- Draw thin diagonal lines, then use these as guides to draw the thick lines shown below.

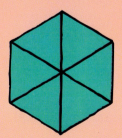 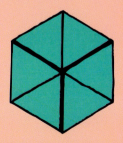 

- Cut along the thick lines to make six identical pieces. Each piece is rhombus-shaped.
- Can you arrange the six pieces to make a 6-pointed star?

JOINING SQUARES

Different shapes can be made by joining sets of identical squares, edge to edge.

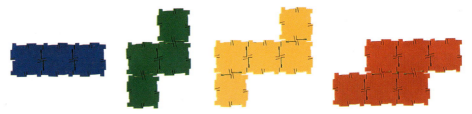

By joining four squares, it is possible to make five different shapes.

CHALLENGE:

How many different 3-square shapes can you make?

TO DO:

Systematically find different 5-square shapes

You need five squares.
- Start by building one of the 4-square shapes shown above.
- Take the fifth square, and place it in different positions around the 4-square shape, each time trying to create a new 5-square shape. These different shapes are possible.

  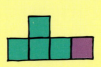

- Do the same for each of the other 4-square shapes, to see how many different 5-square shapes you can find altogether.

CHALLENGE:

The 5-square shapes are called **pentominoes**.

There are twelve possible different pentominoes. Here are eleven. What is the missing pentomino?

CHALLENGE:

In the picture at the top of this page, which of the twelve pentominoes above will fold to make an open cube?

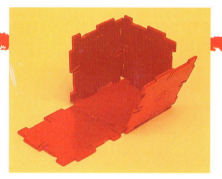

TO DO:

- Make your own set of twelve pentominoes, using squared paper, or card.
- Choose any one pentomino.
- It is possible to use nine of the remaining eleven pieces to make a scale model of your pentomino, three times as big. Try it.

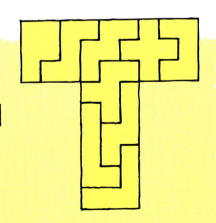

ARRANGEMENTS

The order in which we choose a set of objects creates an **arrangement**. If we choose them in a different order, we create a different arrangement. In many mathematical problems it is useful to be able to find all the different possible arrangements.

If you are using two colours of bricks to make towers of height two, then it is possible to build four different towers.

The four towers show the number of different arrangements of the bricks.

CHALLENGE:

You need two bricks each of three colours. You are to build towers of height two by choosing from these three colours. It is possible to build nine different towers. Can you find them?

CHALLENGE:

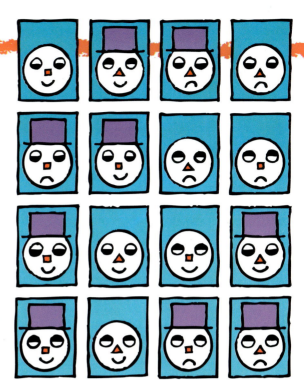

These pictures show different faces. Some are happy, some are sad. Some are looking up, some are looking down. Some have a square nose, some have a triangular nose. Some are wearing a hat, some are not. All the faces should be different, but the artist has made a mistake.

- Two of the faces are identical. Can you spot them?
- One face is missing from the picture. Can you draw it?

The picture shows three numbered cards, 5, 2 and 6, arranged to make a three-digit number.

Six different three-digit numbers can be made with these cards:

| 256 | 526 | 625 |
| 265 | 562 | 652 |

Notice how they are arranged in order, with first '2' hundreds, then '5' hundreds and then '6' hundreds.

TO DO:

- Make these four numbered cards.
- Use the cards to investigate how many different two-digit numbers you can make. Write them down.
- Now investigate different three-digit numbers.
- Finally, see how many four-digit numbers you can make.

CODES

The Morse Code was invented by the American inventor, Samuel Morse, over one hundred years ago. It is a code in which letters of the alphabet are represented by combinations of dots and dashes. The dots and dashes are communicated from one person to another by short and long sounds made by electrical contacts.

Here is the code:

A	● ▬	H	● ● ● ●	O	▬ ▬ ▬	V	● ● ● ▬
B	▬ ● ● ●	I	● ●	P	● ▬ ▬ ●	W	● ▬ ▬
C	▬ ● ▬ ●	J	● ▬ ▬ ▬	Q	▬ ▬ ● ▬	X	▬ ● ● ▬
D	▬ ● ●	K	▬ ● ▬	R	● ▬ ●	Y	▬ ● ▬ ▬
E	●	L	● ▬ ● ●	S	● ● ●	Z	▬ ▬ ● ●
F	● ● ▬ ●	M	▬ ▬	T	▬		
G	▬ ▬ ●	N	▬ ●	U	● ● ▬		

TO DO:

Write your name in Morse Code.

CHALLENGE:

Use some counters (for the dots) and rods (for the dashes). There are four different arrangements using any two symbols.

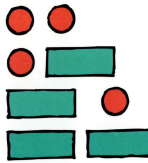

- There are eight different arrangements using three symbols. Can you find them?
- Can you find sixteen different arrangements using four symbols?
- Match a letter of the alphabet from the Morse Code to each arrangement. Are there any which do not match? What could these spares codes be used for?

Braille is a printing code for the blind, invented by a Frenchman, Louis Braille, in 1833. Each letter is represented by an arrangement of spots in a 3 by 2 rectangular shape, and is felt as a bump on the page.

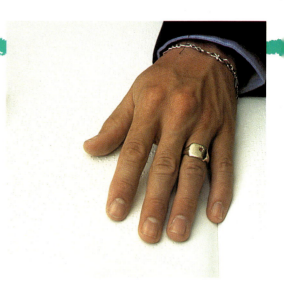

Here is the code:

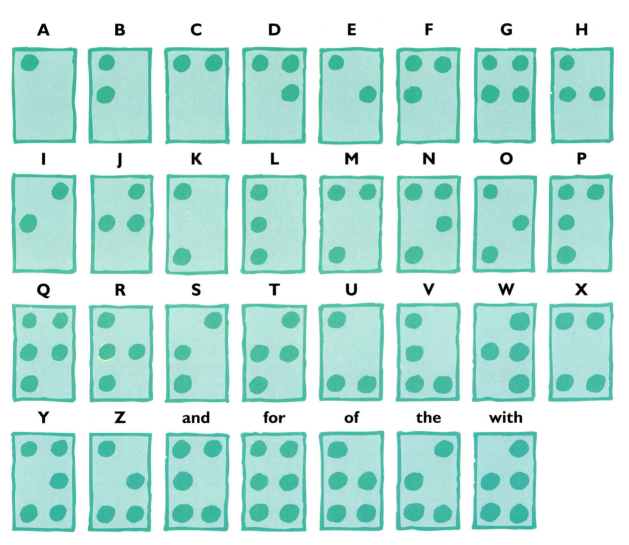

Notice that, as well as the letters of the alphabet, some words also have a Braille code. *Why is this?*

13 ODDS AND EVENS

There are many patterns in odd and even numbers. When whole numbers are written in sequence, they alternate odd, even, odd, even . . .

1 *2* **3** *4* **5** *6* **7** *8* **9** *10* **11** *12* **13** ...

When two numbers are added together, there is a pattern in the oddness or evenness of the total. *Can you see any pattern in the sums below?*

EVEN + EVEN

(2) + (4) = (6)

(6) + (8) = (14)

(12) + (26) = (38)

EVEN + ODD

(4) + [5] = [9]

(10) + [1] = [11]

(8) + [1] = [9]

ODD + EVEN

[3] + (6) = [9]

[5] + (32) = [37]

[11] + (14) = [25]

ODD + ODD

[7] + [11] = (18)

[3] + [1] = (4)

[5] + [9] = (14)

If, instead of adding, we subtract, then the patterns are like this.

EVEN – EVEN

(12) – (4) = (8)

(16) – (6) = (10)

(8) – (2) = (6)

EVEN – ODD

(10) – [1] = [9]

(6) – [3] = [3]

(12) – [7] = [5]

ODD – EVEN

[9] – (2) = [7]

[7] – (6) = [1]

[15] – (4) = [11]

ODD – ODD

[13] – [3] = (10)

[9] – [5] = (4)

[11] – [9] = (2)

TO DO:

- Copy this addition table.
- Colour the squares green which show the result of adding two odd numbers, and of adding two even numbers.
- Colour the squares red which show the result of adding one odd and one even number.
- What patterns can you see?

+	1	2	3	4	5	6
1	2	3	4	5	6	7
2	3	4	5	6	7	8
3	4	5	6	7	8	9
4	5	6	7	8	9	10
5	6	7	8	9	10	11
6	7	8	9	10	11	12

These are the rules for addition and subtraction of odd and even numbers.

Addition		
+	Odd	Even
Odd	Even	Odd
Even	Odd	Even

Subtraction		
–	Odd	Even
Odd	Even	Odd
Even	Odd	Even

We can explore patterns in multiplication in the same way.

EVEN x EVEN

2 × 6 = 12
6 × 4 = 24
4 × 8 = 32

EVEN x ODD

4 × 3 = 12
8 × 1 = 8
10 × 5 = 50

ODD x EVEN

5 × 2 = 10
7 × 10 = 70
3 × 6 = 18

ODD x ODD

3 × 7 = 21
5 × 5 = 25
1 × 11 = 11

Here is the multiplication table and the rules for multiplying odd and even numbers.

Multiplication		
x	Odd	Even
Odd	Odd	Even
Even	Even	Even

x	1	2	3	4	5	6
1	1	2	3	4	5	6
2	2	4	6	8	10	12
3	3	6	9	12	15	18
4	4	8	12	16	20	24
5	5	10	15	20	25	30
6	6	12	18	24	30	36

CHALLENGE:

Two different numbers are both between 1 and 10. When they are multiplied together, the result is an odd number greater than 40. What could they be?

14 MULTIPLES PATTERNS

When you multiply numbers by 4, then the results are called the **multiples** of 4. The multiples of 4 are: 4, 8, 12, 16, 20, 24, 28 and so on.

The multiples of different numbers make different patterns when they are highlighted on a hundred square.

Multiples of 4

1	2	3	4	5	6	7	8	9	10
11	12	13	14	15	16	17	18	19	20
21	22	23	24	25	26	27	28	29	30
31	32	33	34	35	36	37	38	39	40
41	42	43	44	45	46	47	48	49	50
51	52	53	54	55	56	57	58	59	60
61	62	63	64	65	66	67	68	69	70
71	72	73	74	75	76	77	78	79	80
81	82	83	84	85	86	87	88	89	90
91	92	93	94	95	96	97	98	99	100

The multiples of 4 make a chequered pattern.

CHALLENGE:

On the square we can colour 50 multiples of 2 and 25 multiples of 4. How many multiples of 5 could we colour?

TO DO:

Make your own hundred square and highlight patterns for the multiples of 7 and 8.

Multiples of 9

The multiples of 9 make a pattern of sloping lines.

1	2	3	4	5	6	7	8	**9**	10
11	12	13	14	15	16	17	**18**	19	20
21	22	23	24	25	26	**27**	28	29	30
31	32	33	34	35	**36**	37	38	39	40
41	42	43	44	**45**	46	47	48	49	50
51	52	53	**54**	55	56	57	58	59	60
61	62	**63**	64	65	66	67	68	69	70
71	**72**	73	74	75	76	77	78	79	80
81	82	83	84	85	86	87	88	89	**90**
91	92	93	94	95	96	97	98	**99**	100

CHALLENGE:

Look at the sloping lines of multiples of 3.

1	2	**3**	4	5	**6**	7	8	**9**	10
11	**12**	13	14	**15**	16	17	**18**	19	20
21	22	23	**24**	25	26	**27**	28	29	**30**
31	32	**33**	34	35	**36**	37	38	**39**	40
41	**42**	43	44	**45**	46	47	**48**	49	50
51	52	53	**54**	55	56	**57**	58	59	**60**
61	62	**63**	64	65	**66**	67	68	**69**	70
71	**72**	73	74	**75**	76	77	**78**	79	80
81	82	83	**84**	85	86	**87**	88	89	**90**
91	92	**93**	94	95	**96**	97	98	**99**	100

- Look at the line which contains the numbers 93, 84, 75, etc. One number in this line is the 'odd one out'. Can you find it and give a reason?
- Which number is the 'odd one out' in the line which contains the numbers 96, 87, 78, etc.
- Do the other lines have an 'odd one out'?

31

MULTIPLICATION PATTERNS

This is the times 4 multiplication table, and the units digit for each multiple.

$$1 \times 4 = 4$$
$$2 \times 4 = 8$$
$$3 \times 4 = 12$$
$$4 \times 4 = 16$$
$$5 \times 4 = 20$$
$$6 \times 4 = 24$$

What are the next four lines in the table?
Can you see a pattern in the sequence of units digits?

TO DO:

Write down some more multiples of 4, beyond 40, and check that the pattern continues.

The multiples of 2 are: 2, 4, 6, 8, 10, 12, 14, 16, 18, 20 . . .
Their units digits are: 2, 4, 6, 8, 0, 2, 4, 6, 8, 0 . . .
Notice that the same set of five digits is repeated (2, 4, 6, 8, 0), but in a different order.

CHALLENGE:

Can you find some other multiples whose units digits make a repeating pattern of the same five digits?

1	2	3	4	5	6	7	8	9	10
2	4	6	8	10	12	14	16	18	20
3	6	9	12	15	18	21	24	27	30
4	8	12	16	20	24	28	32	36	40
5	10	15	20	25	30	35	40	45	50
6	12	18	24	30	36	42	48	54	60
7	14	21	28	35	42	49	56	63	70
8	16	24	32	40	48	56	64	72	80
9	18	27	36	45	54	63	72	81	90
10	20	30	40	50	60	70	80	90	100

There are many patterns in a multiplication square.

Can you see any pattern in the ninth row? What about the fifth column? Can you see any patterns in the other rows and columns?

Notice that the number 24 appears in an arc formation.
Can you see any other numbers in an arc formation?
What is the pattern in the numbers along the diagonal?
Notice the symmetrical pattern each side of the diagonal.

CHALLENGE:

- Draw a 10 x 10 square.
- Write the units digit of each number in the multiplication square.
- When you have completed it, find as many patterns as you can.

			4						
			8						
			2						
			6						
5	0	5	0	5	0	5	0	5	0
			4						
			8						
			2						
			6						
			0						

NINES

The multiples of 9 have many patterns.

In the number square, the multiples of 9 make a sloping line pattern.

The first ten multiples of 9 are: 9, 18, 27, 36, 45, 54, 63, 72, 81 and 90. *Can you see any pattern in the numbers?* Look at the pattern in the units digit, and in the tens unit.

1	2	3	4	5	6	7	8	9	10
11	12	13	14	15	16	17	18	19	20
21	22	23	24	25	26	27	28	29	30
31	32	33	34	35	36	37	38	39	40
41	42	43	44	45	46	47	48	49	50
51	52	53	54	55	56	57	58	59	60
61	62	63	64	65	66	67	68	69	70
71	72	73	74	75	76	77	78	79	80
81	82	83	84	85	86	87	88	89	90
91	92	93	94	95	96	97	98	99	100

TO DO:

Use your fingers and thumbs to multiply by 9

• Spread out your fingers and thumbs, imagining that they are numbered like this:

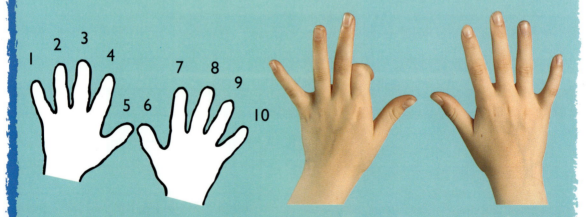

• To multiply 9 by 4, bend the fourth finger.
• Then count the fingers to the left and right: 3 and 6, 36. So 9 multiplied by 4 is 36.
• Use your fingers and thumbs to multiply other numbers by 9.

TO DO:

- Make a list of the next ten multiples of 9: 99, 108, 117 and so on.
- Describe any patterns you notice.

9 18 27 36 45 54 63 72 81 90

Notice that 18 and 81 are the reverse of each other, and that 27 and 72 are the reverse of each other. *Can you see any more patterns like this?*

Notice also that 18 + 81 = 99 and 27 + 72 = 99.
Do the other pairs make the same pattern?

Another pattern in the multiples of 9 is found by adding their digits. For example, 27 is a multiple of 9, and its digit sum is 2 + 7 = 9.

FACTBOX											
Multiples of 9	2	18	27	36	45	54	63	72	81	90	99	108
Digit sum	9	9	9	9	9	9	9	9	9	9	9	9

The factbox shows the digit sums for other multiples of 9. *What do you notice? What do you think will be the digit sum for other multiples of 9?*

CHALLENGE:

- Can you see a quick way of deciding if a number can be divided by 9?
- Six of these numbers can be divided by 9. Which ones?

340   1008   135   72   89   504
       234   421   163   126

17 NUMBER SHAPES

The first pegboard contains 16 pegs arranged in a square shape. So 16 is called a **square number**. *Which square numbers do the other pegboards illustrate?*

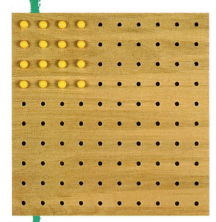
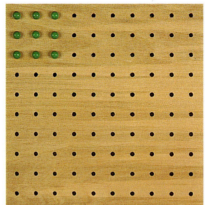
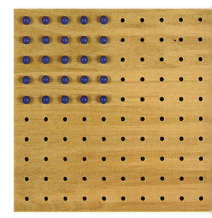

15 balls can be arranged in an equilateral triangle formation, like this. So 15 is called a **triangular number**.

Which triangular numbers do these tins illustrate?

In order, the square numbers are:

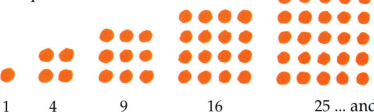

1   4   9   16   25 ... and so on.

In order, the triangular numbers are:

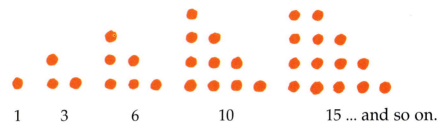

1   3   6   10   15 ... and so on.

Notice that if you choose two consecutive triangular numbers and put them together, you make a square number.

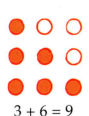

3 + 6 = 9

10 + 15 = 25

Here are some **rectangular numbers**:

8   10   12

CHALLENGE:

How many rectangular numbers can you find between 10 and 20? How many between 20 and 30?

CALENDARS

If you look closely at a calendar, you can discover many different number patterns.

September						
M	Tu	W	Th	F	Sa	Su
			1	2	3	4
5	6	7	8	9	10	11
12	13	14	15	16	17	18
19	20	21	22	23	24	25
26	27	28	29	30		

6	7
13	14

2	3
9	10

Look at these two 2 x 2 squares.
Notice that in the first square, the numbers on the diagonals both have the same total, 20.

$$6 + 14 = 20$$
$$7 + 13 = 20$$

In the second square, also, the numbers on the diagonals both have the same total, 12.

$$2 + 10 = 12$$
$$3 + 9 = 12$$

TO DO:

Are the diagonal totals always the same for a 2 x 2 square on a calendar? Find a calendar and try it out for this month.

In the first square, the numbers in the columns have totals of 19 and 21.

$$6 + 13 = 19$$
$$7 + 14 = 21$$

In the second square, the numbers in the columns have totals of 11 and 13.

$$2 + 9 = 11$$
$$3 + 10 = 13$$

TO DO:

Is the total in the second column always two more than the total in the first column?

Choose some more 2 x 2 squares and find out.

38

TO DO:

Look at the 3 x 3 square on this calendar.

March						
M	Tu	W	Th	F	Sa	Su
	1	2	3	4	5	6
7	8	9	10	11	12	13
14	15	16	17	18	19	20
21	22	23	24	25	26	27
28	29	30	31		.	

- Check the totals of the numbers in each diagonal.
- Check the total of the numbers in the middle row.
- Check the total of the numbers in the middle column.
- Choose a different 3 x 3 square and look for patterns in these totals.

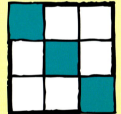 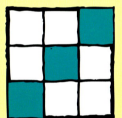 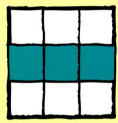 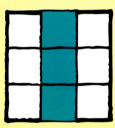

CHALLENGE:

- Choose a 3 x 3 square on the calendar above.
- Find the total of the four corner numbers.
- Find the total of the four 'centre side numbers'.

 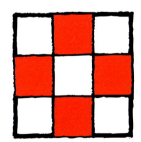

- Can you spot any pattern in these totals?
- Can you spot a relationship between the totals and the centre number?

19 CURVES FROM STRAIGHT LINES

If a ball is thrown into the air from one person to another, the path the ball takes is called a **parabola**. The word 'parabola' comes from a Greek word meaning 'thrown'.

A parabola can be drawn by drawing a pair of angled straight lines of the same length. The lines are marked with equally spaced points, and then numbered. Notice that the numbering is in a different direction on each line. Straight lines are drawn to join the two points numbered '1', the two points numbered '2', and so on. The result is a parabola. As the angle between the lines changes, so the shape of the parabola changes.

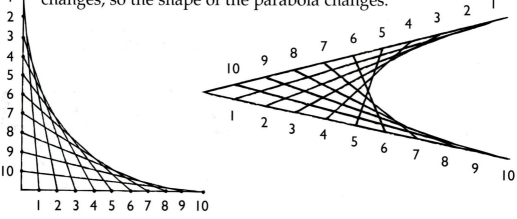

Interesting patterns can be created by extending this method to points marked on the sides of a triangle.

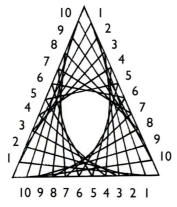

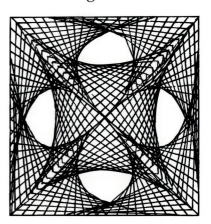

TO DO:

Draw some of these patterns, then invent some new ones of your own.

40

Another way of drawing curves from a set of straight lines is to start with a circle. The circle is marked with a set of equally spaced points. Here there are 36. This can be done by drawing round a 360° protractor and marking a point every 10°. These points are first numbered from 1 to 36, and then again from 37 to 72. Each point is joined to its double. Point 1 is joined to 2, 2 to 4, 3 to 6, 4 to 8, and so on.

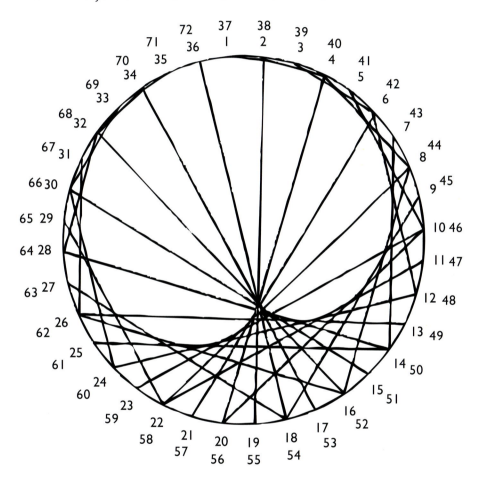

The result is a beautiful pattern known as a **cardiod**. Cardiology is the study of heart disease. A cardiograph is an instrument used to measure heart movements. A cardiod is a heart-shaped curve.

TO DO:

Draw your own cardiod.

CIRCLE DESIGNS

Many patterns can be created with circles, by marking a set of equally spaced points around the circle. The circle below has six equally spaced points. The points are joined with thin lines as shown.

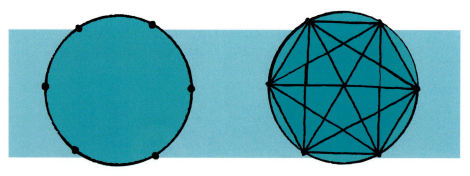

The thin lines can now be used as guides to create different designs.

Are any of these patterns symmetrical?

TO DO:

Draw your own circle with six equally spaced points

- Draw round a 360° protractor, and then mark points every 60°.
- Draw thin lines to join the points, then use them to create your own designs.

This circle pattern is constructed from eighteen equally spaced points. A straight line is drawn to join two points which are six spaces apart.

The final pattern shows another circle inside the first circle.

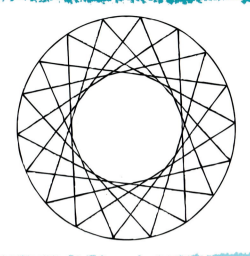

TO DO:

Try this yourself. You can draw round a circular protractor, marking points every 20°, to give eighteen equally spaced points.

If you mark any number of equally spaced points round a circle, then join each point to every other point, the result is known as a Mystic Rose.

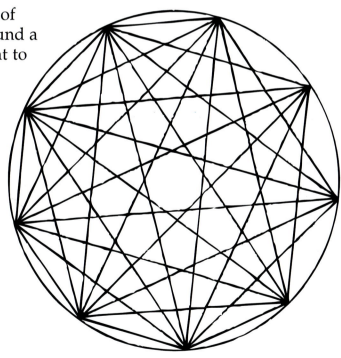

CHALLENGE:

Choose your own number of equally spaced points and draw your own Mystic Rose. See if it creates a circle in the centre.

GLOSSARY

arrangement	The order in which we choose a set of numbers or objects.
cardiod	A heart-shaped curve.
centre of rotation	The point about which a shape or object turns.
clockwise	Turning in the direction in which clock hands move.
congruent	Congruent shapes are identical in size and shape.
diameter	The length of a chord of a circle which passes through the centre.
equilateral triangle	A triangle with two sides equal in length.
hexagon	A polygon with six sides.
isosceles triangle	A triangle with two sides equal in length.
kite	A quadrilateral with two pairs of adjacent equal sides.
line of symmetry	The line which divides the two matching halves of a shape with line symmetry.
line symmetry	Shapes and patterns have line symmetry when they have two matching halves, one a reflection of the other.
multiples	The results of a multiplication table.
number spiral	An arrangement of numbers in a spiral on a square grid.
order of rotational symmetry	The number of times a rotated shape makes its own image when rotated for one complete turn.
parabola	A curve traced by the path of a ball when thrown in the air.
pattern	An arrangement of shapes, numbers or colours.
pentagon	A polygon with five sides.
pentagram	A shape made by joining the diagonals of a regular pentagon.
pentomino	A shape made by joining five equal squares.
radius	The distance from the centre of a circle to its boundary.

rectangular number	If a set of counters can be arranged in a rectangle pattern, then the number of counters used is called a rectangular number.
reflection	A mirror image.
reflective symmetry	Line symmetry.
regular polygon	A polygon in which all angles are the same size and all sides are the same length.
rhombus	A 'squashed' square, or a parallelogram with all four sides the same length.
right angle	A quarter turn.
rotation	A turn about a central point.
rotational symmetry	Shapes have rotational symmetry if, when rotated for one complete turn, they make their own image more than once.
spiral	A curve that moves out from a central point.
square number	If a set of counters can be arranged in a square pattern, then the number of counters used is called a square number, or it is the result of multiplying a number by itself.
symmetrical	A shape is symmetrical if it has line symmetry.
tessellate	Shapes tessellate if they fit snugly without leaving any spaces between them.
triangular number	If a set of counters can be arranged in an equilaterail triangle pattern, then the number of counters used is called a triangular number.

INDEX

ANSWERS

p5

Challenge:

2	4	6	8	<u>10</u>	<u>12</u>	
3	6	9	12	<u>15</u>	<u>18</u>	
5	10	15	20	<u>25</u>	<u>30</u>	
56	48	40	32	<u>24</u>	<u>16</u>	
1	2	4	8	<u>16</u>	<u>32</u>	
1	4	9	16	<u>25</u>	<u>36</u>	
1	3	6	10	<u>15</u>	<u>21</u>	
1	1	2	3	5	<u>8</u>	<u>13</u>

Challenge:

1	5	10	10	5	1
1	6	15	20	6	1

p7

p8

p9

Challenge:
A and K; B and M; E and L; H and F; C and I. Odd one out is J.

p11

All the lines of symmetry pass through the centre of the circle.

p12

The wheel will make its own image 12 times.

p13

Challenge: Order of rotational symmetry: 3, 4, 8, 4, 4, 4

p14

have line symmetry.

have line symmetry.

All the 4-tile patterns have rotational symmetry.

have rotational symmetry.

p17

Squares and regular octagons; squares, equilateral
triangles and regular hexagons

p19

The odd and even numbers make a chequered pattern.
The square numbers make a diagonal pattern.
The multiples of 4 make a symmetrical pattern about the
diagonal from top left to bottom right.
Every other diagonal line contains even numbers.

p21

Hexagons, 4; squares, 8; squares, 5; squares, 6;
pentagons, 5; hexagons, 5

p22 There are 2 different 3-square shapes.

p23 **Challenge:**
The missing pentomino is:

Challenge:

p25 **Challenge:**

To do:
23, 25, 28, 32, 52, 82, 35, 53, 38, 83, 58, 85.
235, 253, 258, 285, 238, 283, 325, 352, 358, 385, 328,
382, 523, 532, 538, 583, 528, 582, 823, 832, 853, 835,
825, 852.
There are 24 possible arrangements.

p29 **Challenge:**
7 and 9

p30 **Challenge:**
20 multiples of 5

p31 **Challenge:**
30, the others have digits which total 12; 60

p32 7 x 4 = 28
8 x 4 = 32
9 x 4 = 36
10 x 4 = 40   The digits 4, 8, 2, 6, 0 are repeated.

p33 Ninth row contains multiples of 9. Fifth column contains
multiples of 5. All numbers in rows and columns are
multiples of the first number in that row or column.
4, 6, 8, 9, 10, ...
All numbers in the diagonal are square numbers.

p35 **To do:**
99, 108, 117, 126, 135, 144, 153, 162, 171, 180
All the digits add up to 9.

Challenge:
1008, 234, 135, 72, 504, 126

p36 The other pegboards illustrate 9 and 25.
The tins illustrate 3, 6 and 10.

p37 **Challenge:**
Between 10 and 20: 12, 14, 15, 16, 18.
Between 20 and 30: 21, 22, 24, 25, 26, 27, 28

p42 All the patterns are symmetrical.